Cornflakes In My Water

Trayzon Akanaton

iUniverse, Inc.
New York   Bloomington

iUniverse books may be ordered through booksellers or by contacting:

iUniverse
1663 Liberty Drive
Bloomington, IN 47403
www.iuniverse.com
1-800-Authors (1-800-288-4677)

Because of the dynamic nature of the Internet, any Web addresses or links contained in this book may have changed since publication and may no longer be valid. The views expressed in this work are solely those of the author and do not necessarily reflect the views of the publisher, and the publisher hereby disclaims any responsibility for them.

ISBN: 978-1-4401-8548-9 (sc)
ISBN: 978-1-4401-8549-6 (ebook)

Printed in the United States of America

iUniverse rev. date: 11/24/2009

This book is dedicated to all those imprisoned.

For My TEEM Player

CONTENTS

CORNFLAKES IN MY WATER

CORNFLAKES IN MY WATER

Picture a child, dreams as immense as the Grand Canyon
Stumbling in poverty's stupor
The only means between a slow death and the dawn of living
Breathing merely to alleviate the pain holding his breath brings
Wishing for wings to imitate the bat
Dreading to be seen; soaring higher than cloud nine
A place where only life can take him
He watches as his older sister fills his soup bowl
With generic cornflakes and tap water
Knowing that this isn't living
Good thing though, his imagination is as colorful as any kaleidoscope
Rendering circumstances barely bearable
A roach races across the cold floor
The boy traps it in cupped hands that must have seemed like a giant's
It ran in circles, from left to right, before holding still, accepting its fate
Instead of killing it, the child explains how he hates having to eat
his cereal
With water and not milk like the kids in the television
Oftentimes he became one of those kids
The boy dips his fingers into the small bowl and drops a soggy
cornflake onto the floor
The roach, instead of accepting the gift, bolts for dear life

SULLEN MOUNTAINS

It has taken practice to become Mr. Nonchalant
Luckily I was able to get a jump on the competition
As I began practicing very young
Looking past the facade at the conditioning are the main ingredients
Uncertainty, fear, lack of confidence, fear of appearing weak
Here I find true self; a guy who isn't so heartless or indifferent
Though I laughed and often smiled
It was not necessarily viewed as a weakness
But something more insidious, perhaps even strength
Of course, I'm referring to the street life.
Aside from anger and blatant indifference
I didn't dare verbalize my innermost feelings
The things that make my heart quiver
But I am human, damn it! I am!
Okay, okay I admit that at one point it was difficult for me
To say I love you to family
Mind you, I did think it; so there!
So next time you are talking and I appear distant
Don't be so quick to bash me
Perhaps my dog really did die

SOFT STONES

One evening in the projects
While sitting on the bottom step inside our apartment
I couldn't have been any older than seven or eight
My father rushed in bleeding
He stood over the kitchen sink
Washing the dark blood from his left bicep where he had been stabbed
After holding his arm under the running water he turned to face me
Making sure that the reddish pink wound was visible
He said with a smirk, "See, don't you cry!"

NAVIGATING SHIT

An epitome of heaven
Given a decaying vehicle for travel
Such a claustrophobic space
So confining this human body
Often battered and scathed
Disrespected and dumped on
This is only some of what I've done to self
When taking selflessness to the extreme
Navigating, dodging external drama
Only to slip and fall on my own shit
Some navigating, huh

A LOVE BORNE

A manifestation of positive energy
The epitome of positivity
The very energy that motivates my inhale
Once I exhale, it's what I inhale – for real
It takes refuge in my soul, my heart its sanctuary
It's scary thinking of breathing without this energy I believe in
In a single breath it makes me smile
Wow, in the same exhalation could make me cry...
My only ally; I'd rather die than not know it
Reveal my love than not show it
For it's the breath I breathe
In this web I weave
This energy has gotten the best of me
Didn't know I could be happy here
This positive energy is the stratosphere of my atmosphere
Would give up weed if this energy agreed to cultivate my seed
Hear my plea, as I speak the blood of my emotions
See, it's the water in the ocean...
Like moisturizer to skin so dry without it may die!
Damn. Should she have only smiles to give I'd accept 'em as we embrace
Then convert into the electromagnetic spectrum
Didn't know I could be happy here
Thank God for the stratosphere in my atmosphere.
Could I be the destiny that enhances the life of this energy?
Or could I be the motivation that persuades this energy to be the curve
of my smile? Don't have much to give in terms of money, but like kids
What I have to give exceeds monetary value; transcends time's patience
Like expensive wine this energy I could never afford
So I spent time bettering my mind
For the time it knocks at my door; now ready thanking God
This positivity I adore – a love borne

THE ME FACTOR

Like words divinely placed, I'm poetry manifest
Like the bulging hillside, I too am the strong silent type; unwavering
in my resolve
A cracking of my heart like that of atoms belies many premonitions.
Beneath the rugged walls of my volcano, truth, purity and perhaps
Fractions of the cosmos are the seat of my essence
Totally selfless and only selfish in time of assertion
I'm the ink on these pages; the roots of plants and weeds alike
I'm a must have; a necessity in this life. I am laughter, plus the curve
of her smile
I am good days and bad and as complex as contradiction – my profile
Should I emulate the sun, it's only because I admire what it inspires
me to be
Forever vigilant, watchful, comforting and quiet
A provider of light in the hearts of mankind
Should I imitate the wind, know that my end is to be seldom seen yet
forever felt
The many welts from life's belt have hardened my bones
Triggered an endless boiling of my blood, like the chemical reaction of
an isotope
So as my purpose is to conceive goals
I cease to loathe, then witness my anger convert into a tool for
betterment
Becoming is what I am

PART ONE OF THIRD EAR

Tears untamed, countless streams flow uncontrollably
My nasal passage fills with thick mucus, before blowing it into a wad
of tissue
Another deep breath and a hole is blown through
My fingers are slimy and I don't give a damn
Like a scared puppy, my eyes occasionally land on the cell door
Careful that no one sees me this way
The hurt and guilt, behind my breastbone, has filled to capacity
Bubbling over like molten lava; hot tears sliding down the rough wall
of my volcano
I struggle to silence these cries for fear of my neighbor discovering my
humanity
Oh, how much I want to yell out, "Aggghhh…!"
But I pull at my shirt and bed sheets instead
And because I hold back my forehead begins to throb
And it feels as though the top of my head is about to pop open like a
heated teapot
Creeping over my top lip is a faint taste of sea
Ten minutes have passed since receiving mail with pictures of my aunt
and mother
The boundless blue sky in contrast with their dark skin is jazz manifest
One look into their faces has completely shattered the walls of my
nonchalance
I feel like a small child, alone and uncertain
I've spent the bulk of my life in a whirlwind genocide
Selfish and inconsiderate of Mom's love
And like every mom, she only wanted the best for her child, me
And though I couldn't shake the terrible stench of gang-banging, she
never judged me
But would always tell me that I could be successful at whatever I
chose to do
And once again, Mom was right.
Here I am at thirty-two with three sixteen-year-old bullet scars against
my body
My skin complete with graffiti

My sleep punctured by post-traumatic stress, inside prison
A 'successful' gang-banger, indeed, who has escaped no reaps life throws back
Nope, not even death
For with so many loved ones having been murdered
I too have died multiple deaths in return
Only to go on living the stress of many centuries past

PART TWO OF THIRD EAR

So many precious years I have spent in the thick of street life
Years that were the seat of my mom's worries
Years that kept her awake late nights, hoping I was okay
While half-expecting to receive that heart-wrenching phone call
That I'm sure every mother must dread
For years, I hadn't noticed the toll my decisions had taken on my mom
I was living in the fast lane, at great speeds
Where a delicious meal was impossible to taste; only chewed and
swallowed
I had no time for anyone outside of my gang
I was running at a fast pace attempting to escape circumstance
There wasn't room for a relationship; sex was merely pursued in my
search for heaven
My gang was my God and I its most obedient disciple
Looking at the pictures of my mom I can't but wonder
How many of her gray hairs were I the cause
Who knew that I'd ever be so worthy of blame?!
With pictures in hand, I cry
Desperate to prove that I've finally awakened
That I could make it in this strange existence, minus the lying life
of crime
It has taken me three decades but I've found truth

ESOTERIC

Eyes of blue marble, skin dipped in white chocolate
At first glance, she's innocent
Then more experienced at life's woes than I wanted to believe
She's as sweet as soft rain; her touch as comforting as the tiger's coat
Who is she? Where did she come from?
Surely, only an angelic being could embody such extraordinary gravity
For, her proximity provides me an unknown joy
But perhaps it's Bipolar that compels her to snap, cracking my
confidence
Reducing me to a mere ant
Even then, with hurt feelings, I'm glad to know her
And each time her lovely eyes fall upon me I'm certain that I am blessed
Though all woman she possesses the inner strength of ancient pillars
I think this is what attracts me most
She stirs so much emotion within me yet I can't help but to grow more
attached
Often times I wonder if we are of kindred spirits
And I know that the both of us would be placing our souls on the line
If we should commit to such a journey
My heart tells me that she's one of life's rarities
And to fully enjoy I must risk vulnerability
In one word she's poetry

WHAT HAVE I GOTTEN?

A sense of self-worth, ability, and compassion
Awareness of my power to influence and affect others
A power I hope to use in pursuit of my dreams
The things I've gotten from this woman sparked a flame within
Illuminating my path plus the murky corners of my internal
Enabling me to better learn self by taking an honest and complete look into me
Today I understand that behavior alone doesn't define the person
She is my impetus, whether she likes it or not
I'm not concerned with the guy she's seeing because he doesn't compare
Nor can he provide the loyalty that she so deserves
I only hope that she sees this and the fact that
Her mere acquaintance clarifies my direction
Through the reflection in her eyes I found me
Her proximity exudes peace; a calm, a protection, a love
For the first time in my existence
I can honestly say that the ability to feel is the most wonderful thing
I can't recall ever wanting to touch and smell someone as much as I do her
I like the way she makes me feel
Because of her I now know the necessity of appreciation
Being without her is difficult
And though I may find other women attractive
It doesn't compare to the way I feel about Baby
And only validates what I already know
She's the only person, like a missing piece to a jigsaw, who may ever complete me
And should our puzzle ever come apart
I'm confident that she and I, with patience and resolve, can piece it back together
Somehow she has rendered my impervious exterior an aquifer
Finding her way to and then slow dancing with my nucleus
It's like I have been running over thick vines entwined
Only to find myself face to face with a rarity not yet discovered by man
An extraordinary orchid of unmatched beauty
A man lost discovers destiny

PILLARS

Two storms a world apart pouring acid-rain onto the lives of two strangers
Chosen by fate, there is no escape for this is the hand life has dealt
Anguish seethes, eating at emotions; each heart builds itself a fortress
Needing protection from what was thought to be harmless
Now aloof for fear of lurking deception, badly seeking space from all
Seizing the moment to allow tears to cleanse; to refresh, rejuvenate…
It will be okay!
And then I met her: curly hair, soft yet strong features
Green eyes that speak a language of their own
Indeed I was intrigued, wanted to reach out and touch her face wasn't sure if she was real
We bonded the way I have with no other
An authentic sista whom I could never disrespect
We stood alone through exclusive storms then dissipated
Bringing her and I together, two shattered lives that have been pieced together
Scars reside inside her eyes, her smile brighter than her reflections
There are no lies between us; our relationship is based on companionship
We connect through realism – the rest will come later
I want to take my time with this one
I like how we are able to stand strong in our individual capacities
Pillars in our own right
Should either of our knees weaken, we'd just lean on the other
After all, relationships aren't always fifty-fifty; sometimes they are sixty-forty.

ONYX AND PEARL

Contrary yet kindred spirits
A subset of qualities superimposed
Power through misfortune, withstanding the unthinkable
Naturally rare, synthetically common
Cultivated through the serendipity of nature
At once removed and at one with their origins
When brought together their stark contrasts apparent
When apart the inexplicable magnetism drawing them together palpable
Melding together as dark chocolate into white at searing temperature
The collective pain no longer recognizable
They complement one another like the corners of a drawer
Fragments fitting into one another's innermost crevices
From shiny surfaces to the tiny grain of sand that is rooted in half
They become solitary

SEASONED RED BEANS

Love is life, pure
As a boy I'd watch Grandma tending garden
Plump grapes, strawberries, squash created an exclusive existence
A few feet away atrocities manifest
But her garden didn't seem to mind
This was her creation; her baby
A purity – essence of which undisturbed
She'd enter, the strawberries would fatten, the grapevine shift about on windless days
All seemed to compete for her attention
I watched in awe as she knelt examining a patch of red beans
Even when yelling at my antics Grandma was quietly generating a peaceful air
A country girl at heart, constructing a small replica in the big city
Nostalgia I suppose
Sweaty, dirty, out of breath
I entered the kitchen off the rear yard and was ushered to the restroom's basin
In passing, aromatic dishes dangled before my famished self
At the table on my plate steaming seasoned red beans reclining in their own juices
I knew at once from where they'd come
I tried a few and knew Grandma was underappreciated
The rest went inside my pocket for the bum in front of the market
I'll give them to him tomorrow

THE TIME IS NOW!

It is funny really, I mean, to be standing in these shoes
You see, not in a million years would I have thought that one day
I'd evolve from a hoodlum, wanting nothing more than a low rider,
into a man (finally)
Of drive and ambition, desiring the fruit of an honest day's work
Tired of the spoils of illicit business
For I'm that very person who deified material possessions
And their most easily accessible route
But the consequences have proven too costly; life far too short.
So I find myself battling old habits, while attempting to embrace
new ones
But how would a person know if he has actually changed?
This question I ask myself remains unanswered
Perhaps, it's the unsuspected struggle that came with change that
triggered such inquiry
I don't know, though I am certain that life had never been so difficult
Until the moment that I effected change
I hadn't realized the deep conditioning I had undergone
That was until I dared to venture outside the norm
Oftentimes I want to throw my hands up and say, "To hell with it!"
Then, again, I'm reminded of what I don't want and have learnt a
valuable thing
Change can take a lifetime
A constant reminder of my distaste for my current situation
Making my goals, both short and long term, my focal point is what
keeps me going
Slushing through the thick grime of my downs
When my days are meek and my patience thin
Hope dwindles like a stick of margarine in a frying pan
The thing that gets me most is when people attempt to push my buttons
And because this was a major problem for me in the past
I have taught myself to dismantle, disconnect, and discard said buttons
So that my anger can no longer be used as strings by the pseudo
puppet master
But I must reiterate, the only way this is possible is through my goals

Actually wanting something righteous out of life
Without goals how can I possibly have any direction?
How can my life ever have any meaning if I don't set positive goals,
seeking purpose?
I believe this existence transcends power and money
Give me power over self and richness in spirit and I'm good

OF CRIMINAL MIND

As long as we remain cynical, visionless, and jealous of one another
And as long as we continue to fight our neighbors, steadfast in illusory
justifications
Having no foundation in reason, logic, or moral law – misdirected
aggression
Sparked by those who control the world commerce
Indirectly nourishing our present repressive state
We, the constituents, of the destitute caste, will forever fail in attaining
the goals
That we have been hoodwinked into believing *the game* will one day
provide
We'll remain stagnant with sealed minds
And because it is within our nature as human beings to imitate
We will continue to condition our posterities
Into this very cycle to which we have become victim
There is nothing wrong with desires of striking it rich
(That is the rationale for our life of crime, right?)
But there is everything wrong with not wanting to open our minds
Constantly seeking the easy way out, not wanting to do the required
labor
Pointing the finger, blaming others for our self-imposed shortcomings
Being that we're not content with the quality of our lives
Lacking the knowledge of the source of our next dollar, poverty
stricken
And because the cares our neighbor holds reflect those of our own
Reminding us of the discontent that we so endeavor to escape
By way of mind altering substances, we wage war
Not because we actually share an enmity or hatred for one another
But because of our position on the economic ladder
Taking the ill feelings imposed by our socio-economic positions
And projecting them onto each other
Whenever we are within the solidarity of our kindred, we speak in
delusion
Conveying our belief that this time we are sure that we can turn an
ounce of dope into a million bucks

Because this time we're going to do it differently

And we may succeed, but what happens when the Feds are kicking down our doors

Scaring our babies and taking everything we've hustled for? Who is the real winner? Open your mind, big homie, because like Vegas the game was designed for us to lose

So today I take another step towards rehabilitation

In an environment that has yet to be habilitated…it is possible.

THE MASK

You never knew what I was hiding: Admiration, respect, fascination
Lurking beneath so much superfluous drivel
Words unspoken yearning to break free
I wear the mask well
You never knew what I was thinking
When you were close, when you were speaking
Smiling condescendingly, sarcasm dripping from your tongue
Sharp laughter that sliced through my heart like icicles of shattered glass
I wear the mask well
You never knew the pain I felt or saw the tears in the eyes you admire
Convenient moments I turned away from you so you couldn't see your
effect on me
I wear the mask well
You never knew the ache I felt to be near you
To hear the resonance of your voice
To see the genuine gaze you seldom gifted me
To feel your touch
All the while my granite exterior giving contrary signals
My false voice singing a contrary song
I wear the mask well
You never knew the fear that engulfed me
Exposing my carefully guarded thoughts so blatantly black and white
Risking wondering imagining waiting, waiting, waiting
Wondering what you would feel when you glimpsed that power within me
I wear the mask well
You never knew the panic I felt when you turned your back on me
I had split my heart asunder and laid bare its inner view
Only to feel it nonchalantly trampled upon
I stood with oblivious expression frivolous conversation spilling from me
Wilting inside, longing to run to you
I wear the mask well
You never knew the trembling within
When I faced you with open heart no way to hide my feelings
Needing to leak it all but only a trickle revealed through the cracking
of the mask

So much I tried to tell you too much at once I know
You laughed, bringing those icicle shards once again to my heart
Too many words crowding what my spirit wanted to commune
The energy between us overwhelming me, the parameters oppressing me
Sentiments half spoken feelings barely revealed
Another time another place will there ever be, when the mask can be
fully liberated
Sensing your capacity to receive all that lay within; few have been up
to the challenge
The labyrinth of evolution undergone
Kindred spirits, pillars, complements, magnets, fragments, solitary
How can these words portray the bond or your capability of wrestling
the mask from me?
You've found a mallet strong enough to demolish it into miniscule
particles

INTELLECTUAL LUST

The popular culture love romance physical concept
Seems like a wispy shadow compared to another bond discovered
What is this frivolity deemed the most vital point
Compared to a potent intractable cerebrally intertwining link
Dangerous it is to underestimate intellectual lust
To neglect this basic need in some more crucial than the basest instinct
For to be intellectually stimulated scintillated titillated
Maneuvers our very core and connects tortuously to our primitive
desires
To be fulfilled intellectually is to be fulfilled sensually
Penetrated and filled and engulfed and inundated into the furthest
alcoves of the thalamus
Dwarfing any concept of love or lust ever conjured in previous
perceptions
Or felt in physical interfacing alone
Energy that makes you tremble quiver liquefy
A force from without and within concurrently
Rendering masks unmasked rationality irrational sanity insane
If ever the interaction were transferred to the physical realm
Could the enormity of the encounter be withstood?
Or would they dissolve into each other with the infinite power
No longer recognizable as separate entities
Just a molten silo of grey matter once contained within these bodies
A blissful spontaneous combustion sending them unwittingly into that
cathartic oblivion
Where they discover their arrogance converted into frivolity

A MOVIE IN MY MIND

Where previous thoughts brought harmony, they now bring painful clichés to mind
This one especially fitting: *Fool me once shame on you fool me twice shame on me*
Foolish blind gullible vulnerable; new adjectives employed
Since sinking into the quagmire of one drunk on his own power
And the award goes to Trayzon, the producer and director of the movie in my mind
Skeptical, cynical, realistic, invincible
More familiar and comfortable descriptions now foreign
You fractured me; my mind my heart my soul my trust my love
So lengthy to heal so swift to damage
The well will run dry again before having a chance to replenish itself fully
Does it matter at all does it does it does it
No, now you'll be free of the burden of words and rants
It's not rocket science, to spew another cliché
It's only poetry after all, just words on paper
Merely outtakes from a movie in my mind, so aptly articulated by you
Installing permanent shards in my heart, hammered in with offers of enticement
Sealed with blame and cruel insults and laughter
Unforgivable insults that wound to my very core
Then you dare question how to show appreciation
Stunned I scramble for my mask to rescue me
Such a rude awakening that you were blind to the cracks
Restored I return to true form and real life and the unexpected
Another without harsh words or deeds who sees clearly
Navigates carefully around those obstructions you impaled
Reveling in the abundance left to give
In a gentle manner never speaking the words I deserve to hear
No the cliché is never spoken, *I told you so*
The quagmire beckoned due to a temporary void now filled by reuniting of soulmates
I am rejuvenated, and I am forgiven
For straying in the movie in my mind

CONFINED, ISOLATED MALE

Gone years minus environmental stimulation
Longing titillation subjected to isolation
Could never be beneath man's frailties
I fall ongoing, I fall in triumphs
Landing heroically amid depression
Pressing confidence's portrait
Atop mask's mask, masking me
Fasting steadfast potent lust consumes rational thought
Pitting self opposite reality
The smile of every woman
Translates into something more
Even common courtesy misconstrued
So beware this confined isolated asexual
For my lack of touch
Left to touch self
Such a feeble attempt at de-flaming lava rock
Readily reclining within a woman's smile
Doesn't matter her eyes failed to be congruent
Confinement turns social mores unrecognizable
Isolation conjures vulnerability
Bursting at the seams

A LION'S SHARE

Hear; hear, for it is time that we took our eyes off the distractions
And placed our sights upon the panorama or bigger picture
In fact, it is necessary if we are to ever develop the awareness it takes
To successfully circumvent the booby traps that have been placed
Within the microcosm of our ghettos
Wars have been waged! Wars that we'd rather not have had materialize
Both within our borders as well as beyond
While the U.S. internal struggles are overt, the true causations remain hidden
From those with a blind consciousness, as planned
Take for instance the supposed war on drugs that has been waged
By the very coterie who, in the past, had overwhelming evidence levied against it
For not only investing in drugs, but for actually supplying the aircraft
Or the shipment of these hazardous chemicals (i.e. contra scandal)!
Do not be fooled, though the faces have changed
The interest of the demagogue remains the same
Recalling the teachings of Machiavelli, politicians are, to a degree, the victims of chance
While they scheme to advance their clandestine political interests
It isn't difficult to understand that in order to oppress a nation
And to maintain that oppression it becomes essential to distract the people
By any means necessary, as long as those means do not interfere with the pocket stuffing
Of the aristocracy; drugs being the most desirable of all distractions
Particularly when placed in low income communities
Because along with the presence of drugs are so many by-products
Such as the illusion of overnight success and the buying of who got it first
Drug addicts, petty drug dealers, dysfunctional families, single parent households
Chemically dependent newborns, school dropouts, stagnation, crime
Eventually those affected will become so victimized by the concoction

24

And so immersed in the small screen that they will totally forget
That they are, indeed, an oppressed people and at some point in time
Will grow to accept having roaches inside their refrigerator
How then can they ever put the gears of oppression into reverse?
They can't
And as a result will gradually slip into a self-suppressive state
At which point the oppressed/self-suppressed will be at each
other's throats
As it is today, minus any genuine casus belli; with the aristocracy
and its covert wars, hidden hands inside mountainous drugs that
makes them all the more wealthy
Facilitating the landing of poisonous chemicals into our communities
(I've yet to meet anyone living in the projects who owns aircraft of
any kind)
With the assumption that we will eagerly and without question
Accept the contaminated lion's share that the lion herself would
never accept.

A LION'S SHARE: A SECOND LOOK

So much have we, convicts, proven to be like the lion that suffers
temporary blindness
Resulting from the poisonous bite of a rattlesnake
Of course, this is where our similarities begin and end
As the lion, once bitten, has enough sense to recognize her loss of
sight as a disadvantage
Causing her to seek asylum to properly care for herself in hopes of
making a full recovery
This is called self-preservation. Many before her have died, only a few
proven resilient. Many of us are asleep on our feet dancing the dance
of disaster, in the misty snake's spell
Falling to our deaths; some righteous, others as slimy as the snake that
bit them
Many more will undoubtedly succumb, with eyes that had long ago
been bandaged
Brilliant minds that we refused to unlock, whose remarkable capacities
we feared
If ever the criminal mind demanded time for a discarding, that time is
now – seize it!
And together may we grab hold of the pendulum and swing to
righteousness
For a man with sight, minus vision, is stagnant
Though the lion's share of wealth is sought
Only large doses of unyielding brick walls are caught
What we have been referring to as poverty here in North America
In light of less fortunate countries, is better described as the pain of
privilege
Those of us in the U.S. working full-time and earning a lousy
minimum wage
Are actually in the top 12% of the richest people in the world
So on a brighter note; we have the lion's share of opportunity, but like
potential
Opportunity is nothing if it isn't being squeezed of its juices
Personally, I don't like merely having potential because that only conveys
That I'm not doing a damn thing
So instead I exchange potential for progress and production; I want results!

FOREVER FORWARD

My uncle said to me years ago after learning that I'd been sent to the
hole for misconduct, "Trayzon, you're not supposed to try to stay in
jail, your goal should be to get out!"
I was in the Los Angeles County jail at the time for possession of a
firearm
And awaiting the next bus to California Youth Authority for parole
violation
The next time I'd see the streets things would go awry, people would
be shot
Lives forever changed; with me decreed to spend the rest of mine in
prison
There's nothing about the monotony of prison life that deserves
bragging rights
It's not easy for me to live with the prospect
Of having to spend the rest of my life behind bars
I don't trust anyone inside this place. How about you?
Have you ever felt that there was no one that you could trust?
Where having friends was synonymous with having enemies at one's
dinner table?
But amongst that which I find problematic, that has to be the minutest
As I don't have a problem with keeping my distance from the cynical
The thing I question most is how I can possibly come up with the most
effective plan
To get myself out of prison, legally, and as soon as possible
For my uppermost fear is becoming content with this environment
I don't refer to this place as my home because it's not
I don't regard the cell as my house because I'm not happy there
I don't pretend that men are women for fear of slipping into that belief
I understand the psychological effects of these seemingly minor yet
common practices
This conditioning, this brainwashing
Finally I've corrected my mind; allowed myself to be open to
different, healthier things
Within my foresight is liberation; so I have dedicated my strengths to
this pursuit

At present, I live for me and only me
Though far from selfish, it is necessary that I put me first
Because I'm aware that if I'm to be successful at giving the powers
that be back their unsolicited life sentence
Then I must take action on my own behalf
Because the homies are not going to do it, and my mother is poor.
I believe in me! And I believe that by putting everything into my pursuit
I will indeed catch up with as well as capture my liberation
This is my unwavering determination in the center of a windy chaos
Should I share these ideals with you, understand them outlandish not
And that you, too, could fight the contentment of prison life
Giving rise to an unmatched desire for your own freedom
I've always had hope but always felt that I'd been missing a certain
ingredient
Consequently, it didn't take long for me to despair
Self-scrutiny as well as that of those around me, taught me that
Having all the hope in the world doesn't matter as hope is hopeless
without a fight
Without a struggle, and an effort, so I've incorporated such into my
resolve.
Additionally, with every exchange between sun and moon
My now deceased uncle's words, my impetus, are another fleck to my
empowerment
I stand strong with the strength of the righteous, generating healthy ideas
With positivity dripping from my pores, like a life-sustaining sap
Hoping to right so many wrongs
I met a guy whose heart I knew was pure and began to relay to him
my perspectives
Regarding this pseudo-heaven, this authentic hell
And my will to fight for a better position in life
He was taken aback and said I was the first he's ever heard speaking in
such a context
I let him know that though my goals may not be of the norm
I must speak to him from the heart because of my desire to win
However far from ordinary my perspective, I will continue in my
pursuit
Spreading seeds here and there, mindful that in light of prison

environment
My ideas are revolutionary, my thinking is revolutionary
My actions and behaviors are revolutionary
Yesterday's norm is today's passé – I'm going to take the criminal
mind and spin it.

I PUT FEAR IN MY BACK POCKET!

My decision to change put into reverse the desensitizing I'd
conditioned myself with
And gradually I began to feel and care for other people!
Being so hard for so long makes having emotions feel like cowardice
Though I know I'm far from being such, this is exactly the way I feel
when I feel
It's like…it's like I've gone soft, even when I know I haven't
Sometimes, I want to arrest the process of evolution mainly because
I doubt my ability at maintaining humanity; I fear that I will let myself
down
Yet I welcome change in spite of inherent difficulty
I'm learning that true evolution, once set in motion
Is incapable of being arrested, slowed down or even sped up for that
matter
But will continue at its own pace, with no regard for the pace I desire
Until it has carried me to the stage of rebirth
And for that I am glad!

LOVE OR LOYALTY

Is it possible to have one without the other?
I wonder if I choose to practice loyalty over love
Would my significant other feel cheated?
Hopefully not, as loyalty is just as strong, if not stronger
And could I possibly love someone I'm not loyal to?
Or be loyal to someone that I do not love?
If yes, then that may explain why I've hurt those I hold dearest
Perhaps the two are so entwined that I shouldn't attempt to separate
them
While placing loyalty over love and working at securing that first
Because without it love falls fragile
To be broken at the first gust of wind

MORE ON LOVE AND LOYALTY

With further reflection love and loyalty questions can be answered
more succinctly
But never decisively, because the question will always be subjective
Up to the interpretation of each individual's heart
Even when there is a coming together of two halves of a whole;
soulmates if you will
I can love many people in many different ways
Some don't require any loyalty at all in that love
Perhaps only my respect and admiration
I can be loyal to those I don't love because of a shared stake in a
group, gang, or team
However, love mixed with loyalty in a romantic relationship implies
exclusivity
This is a separate issue from the loyalty we feel toward family, friends,
or a gang
Or perhaps what our dog might feel toward us
Love, loyalty, romance, lovemaking, partnership, respect and
exclusivity
These are what make a true love and loyalty one on one relationship
When all these factors are combined nothing surpasses the bond that is
formed
So take your loyalty without love, you can give that to anyone
Take your love without loyalty; you can give that to anyone as well
But you will never achieve the self-actualization
That comes with making love on a mountaintop
With the soulmate that meets all of the above criteria

FINGERS THRU HER HAIR

Put faith in me like I do her
Believe in my dreams, goals and abilities like I do hers
Never stop wanting to look at me like I'll never stop wanting her
Like her I, too, desire to be loved
So why can't we love each other?
Why care what others think?
Just allow our bond to strengthen
So that what we share could be likened to words
Thus never lose its meaning
I've sat and watched for signs revealed
I feel her conveyance is real
Forgive me should I impose, I mean no disrespect
But must admit your smile is so inviting.
I reserve a place for you in my highest regard
My only scheme is to Trayzonize your mind
The subtle way that you hypnotize mine
How do I help her understand that I'm not wit' the game playing?
Unlike the men of her past I appreciate her occupying my corner
Still I feel confused
Mainly because I want to do what's right
Only if she'd provide one last sign
Allowing me the chance to Trayzonize her mind
As she forever hypnotizes mine…
As she forever hypnotizes mine…

REASON TO CELEBRATE

He shivered against the cold, crouching in the brush
With no concept of fear he packed the last of the gun powder into the
service rifle
Death was everywhere; the mere stench made his nostrils flare in
disgust
It had been weeks since he last heard silence
In between the seconds when there was no gunfire there was the boom
of cannon
All the while, eerie screams of the maimed and dying
The year was early 1776; the man's name was John Northrop, a slave
Sent to fight for independence of a foreign land for which two of his
brothers had died
John was also fighting for the freedom of his people and this, more
than anything
Filled him with a burning passion, an unshakable resolve in the face of
adversity
However, he only killed out of necessity
And knew that he could never grow accustomed to such savagery
Many a night he reminded himself of the outcome
Of the man of peace in time of war and the man of war in time of
peace
With the back of his hand, John wiped the pouring rain from his eyes
As he and the five remaining soldiers prepared to move out
The old French rifle resting against his shoulder, stomach growling
A feeling of hopelessness had begun to creep on him, and time and
time again
He had to shake it off, as he watched his platoon die, their supplies
dwindle
But he kept moving forward, even though he didn't fully understand
What independence was that his dedication, his loyalty and diligence
Could possibly bring about his freedom (one way or another)

CHASING SHADOWS

I'm allowing my words the chance to be embraced in the hopes of
being understood
In the event I am no longer here to put them to paper
As I write I feel hopeless and crazy
My world is full of pain, mental anguish and hatred
Although I try to think back to days when life was good to me
The outcome remains the same – a fruitless journey
For I continue to lose myself in the fog of unhappiness
It's like I'm trapped inside a labyrinth where illumination does not
exist; only darkness
My world is no more
Up until now I believed I had a grip on life when life actually had a
grip on me!
I feel eternally stagnant. I can't go on like this!
My today shall come to an end; my tomorrow is no more
I've grown weary of ascending the stairs of life
The mere thought of another step is burdensome
Unable to make up my mind, ambivalence prevails
And I continue to breathe this unpleasant breath in the midst of
confusion
I feel so hopeless and crazy! My compassion seems to be diminishing
at a fast rate
I wonder if there is any hope for me
For I have become a bitter hors d'oeuvre to one voracious beast
Inside its belly are jail cells that offer dementia at the price of sanity
My fight is perpetual; I refuse to give up, still I'm losing.

IF I SHOULD SMILE

Did you hear that? She said that I have a beautiful smile
If that's so then God must have had in mind to fool the world
As he methodically composed my heart, one anticipated piece at a time
I wonder if He smiled while doing so
See, it is my understanding that a smile is the cornerstone of
happiness, joy and the like
From this my smile is distinguished
As a child, I inadvertently mastered the art of smiling
In hindsight, I see my reason for this
Smiling has always been much easier than crying
Not easier in the sense of staying away from that emotion, as a male
But in the sense of the world being readily receptive of the smile
I fear that which I cry for no one understands
So, as I wear this veil of mine
And as I waltz through the depths of pain and misunderstanding
I wail a vicious and horrible cry deep down in the solitude of my internal
And if I should smile, only my kindred, the righteous, will know what
is belied
While the malicious grow trusting of the front
As they become drawn into an abyss of perpetual deception
Maybe, just maybe, before this miracle of God's divorces me to be
with the forever
I'd be obliged to smile a genuinely heartfelt smile
I feel so out of place that I'm not sure when it's appropriate to smile
So I smile all the time; afraid that if I go too long without doing so
That the fluids behind my eyes, submerging my soul
Will make a violent and uncontrollable escape, exposing to the world
My inability to be content within this imbalance
But, if I should smile...

SOLILOQUY

Akanaton: Trayzon, if you were given the opportunity to have no more than three final words with deceased loved ones, what would they be?

Trayzon: You are somebody.

Akanaton: If you held the key to all of life's mysteries would you use it? If so, to what extent?

Trayzon: To a degree, yes. I'd like to know at what point in history did man merge with beast, what caused it and how much longer must we live as one.

Akanaton: Okay. If you had the choice of being anything in the world, what would that be and why?

Trayzon: I'd be a thunder cloud because that's one thing that man cannot distort, destroy or pollute; moreover, I could come crashing down on his evils at will; drowning out his cynical rhetoric with my thunderous roar.

Akanaton: I truly admire your answer. You embody a soul that predates the hills. Answer me this: If as human beings our heads grew an inch with every one thing that we learn, would you prefer to be wise or ignorant?

Trayzon: Put it this way, I'd need a neck brace and shoulder pads.

Akanaton: Say life's order was suddenly put into reverse and the dead began to exist once again, regressing from adult to childhood, childhood to newborn, newborn to fetus; do you think man would fear being unborn the way he fears death?

Trayzon: I would have to say, yes, being aware of man's fear of change. This is a good question because I often hear people saying how they don't want to get old and die or wishing that they could turn back the hands of time.

Akanaton: But what if once reversed the clock fails to stop, thus erasing the present as well as history?

Trayzon: Then clearly man would have proven himself too greedy.

DEAR JUSTICE

It's after two in the morning, four hours since lights out
A guy a few cells away has been banging a hard plastic state issued cup
Against the side of the stainless steel sink in his cell since nine
Tink, tink, tink, tink…
Apparently, the correctional officers refused to provide him toilet paper
Triggering in him a psychotic episode of some kind that has lasted
more than five hours
The skin inside my ears has grown raw from constantly re-adjusting
The makeshift earplugs made of small bits of damp toilet paper
Sleep is unapproachable
I can't help but wonder if you meant well when you sent your
myrmidons
To disrupt my life by heartlessly snatching me from the embrace of
my loved ones
Wrongfully accusing and convicting me of a crime of which I had no
involvement
After all, I am the one who smiled as a child, while inside the
classroom
With my right hand above my heart; facing the flag
Of course, that was long before I knew the truth
That being: Liberty and justice isn't for all, but for a chosen few
The injustice of American justice
When one is born in the lowest stratification of the economic caste
And chooses to exercise his first amendment right to the constitution
So one should be extremely cautious while exercising this right
For if not careful, one will be judged and biased based on one's choice
of clothing
It's so bad that I risk landing in jail each time I step outside my home!
If not for something that I've actually done
Then for that which someone else may be guilty
But, see, the Powers That Be couldn't care any less
As no one gives a damn about the little guy
It's like our society functions on a barbaric pecking order where
morality doesn't exist
In order for you to truly be Justice you should not be flawed, cannot be

tainted!
You claim blindness yet clairvoyance
Lost in the prejudice of the genetic make-up before you
Opposed to focusing on the weighing of facts of my criminal trial
Since I'm not a part of the established order, you've made it so that
Your fruit does not become my lot; seeing only when it behooves you
Leaving generations in your wake, attempting to apply pressure to
their many wounds
What you have done in the Americas is criminal
And will one day face not your Justice but the people's!

PEACHY

Where pain runs deep, smiles tread shallow waters
Coinciding with the foreign being
I mean what I mean, what I'm seeing shouldn't be
I close my eyes allowing the retina my mind conceals to reveal
destiny's lot
Recalling scriptures I forgot, those of the righteous
Eternal illumination in abysmal darkness – my life!
Begging to be sought after; longing to be found.
Disguised in an uproar, with only a half of a lemon to eat
Yesterday my neighbor died of starvation
I mean what I mean
What I'm seeing shouldn't be

MY UTOPIA

Where we rise to the pinnacle of consciousness
Awaken the masses no subliminal nonsense
The ninety-five percent of us who are stuck amidst criminal bullshit
Will have a fit when we open our eyes and take a whiff of the stench
While the remaining five percent rejoice at the sight of a refined people
Lending my voice is taking strides non-lethal
Obliterating the evil that attempts to plant seeds in the hemisphere of
our right cerebral
Extinguish the evil in man maybe then we won't have to pretend to be
homies
But could truly be friends; no phobia, take a chance blend in my Utopia
Where adversaries make amends
I ain't mad at the man but at the man I've been
Now greeting gangs with a nod what's up, Homie, ya'll need a job?
I'm looking for workers to help dismantle the façade
Build in its place the cures of my vision just think
If we all went straight it would put prisons out of business
No more cell time or mere pennies for working
Don't know about you but I'm certain I'm tired of jerking
Off by a step, no more, align our mind with the change in time
Human value over dollar signs, diapers over dollar wine
Become enlightened through the monocle chronicles of Mr. Gilbert
Whispers are like silver and gold; refuse to fold though this world is cold
Holding onto my people against the wind's blow
I opened a book and there were footprints that matched my own
In the dark sand of ancient Egypt
In my perusals I found self as well as a compass
That led me from the cell that had become my abode
 Now I stroll with the confidence of an inevitable sunrise
Severing gun ties embracing bad guys, perfect vision and still blind
My core project words onto canvass like wet paint penetrate my pores
Pain is universal
We'd be the rain that reigns in every storm nourishing Mother Earth
With change comes fear – eradicate it
My Utopia

UNCOVERING DIRT

His reflection in the shattered mirror could be viewed simultaneously
in many ways
The cracked pieces gave a distorted perception, others provided
clearer ones
But had it not been for those cracked, he would not have discerned
inherent flaws
Perhaps that which is seen as bad isn't so bad at all and the negative
derived wherefrom
Depending on one's perception, may actually become a strength, if
placed in context

TO LOVE A JAIL BIRD

Is to commit to monogamy; emotions of mahogany complexion
Reflections of a soul's soul in calm waters
Her fingertips send ripples of joy through the grimiest gutter
She sees past my jail garb, piercing emerald eyes upon a fluttering heart
At a time this jail bird was enraged until the day she appeared then
everything changed
She provided reason not to stray from humanity and to look forward to
crescent moons
I long to squeeze her voluptuousness, afraid that she may never return
to my cage
That so fills me with rage.
Afraid of being alone, so alone…sooo alone!
I feel when I don't feel her warm breath on my neck; yet I've never
been so blessed
She knows what it is to love a jail bird so she loves her jail bird
A loose stitch in society's fabric, she has broken away
Daring to experience a difference providing me a chance to know true
passion
Much stronger than the walls of any prison

A NAME ISN'T JUST A NAME

If Mother had known the hand I'd be dealt
Perhaps, instead of Trayzon she would have named me love
A small word yet with so much weight on its shoulders
Lugging around the world's joys and sorrows
Employed with affection, though sometimes deception
Love demands nothing in its essence
So much is cramped into this little word that I wonder how it has stood
the test of time
It's a clear expression of the ingredients of each of the human's
emotions
That when divinely mixed, couldn't be described otherwise

SHE DON'T WANNA BE WOOED

For centuries I have been bent on proving worthy of your love
At least that's how it feels
Not that I am complaining, in fact, my only complaint would be that
Patience is too demanding and doesn't move fast enough
Sometimes I feel that what we share is similar to Bipolar
Especially when you pull me close only to push me away; the inherent
play of courtship
I play along as only a smitten fool would.
I'm not sure what tomorrow will bring
But am sure of one thing: You are the woman for me
Those other women don't amount to much, as I have aligned with the
divine
Where my destiny was found in line with your heart's desire
Your eyes fall upon me and I tremble
What I feel for you is far from simple, so I struggle to convey it
In the most effective way hoping every ounce of my emotions are
portrayed.
In love I trust
Jumping blindly from the precipice; subjecting myself to vulnerability
Unsure of how my revelations will be perceived
I fear being hurt, yet I need to let you know what's happening inside
my heart
Far too much time elapsed, particularly on games, and for that I accept
blame
All would be fine if only you'd realize that
I'm the guy closest to worthy; of appreciating your essence
And even though I tend to come off as rude
Know that it's indeed a learned part of my personality
Perhaps a side effect of my fine ghetto breeding
Whatever the reason, I don't claim perfection and with that said
Am eager to decrease whatever flaws I may have, if only to suit your
expectations
I feel honored whenever I make you laugh
Your proximity reduces my thoughts to incoherent stutter
Rendering my mind a blank

With this comes pure pleasure so should my rough edges ever rub you
the wrong way
Know that my loyalty is pure, my dedication unwavering, my heart
undivided
Allow me to be the one who prepares your meals, draws your bath
I want to be your lover and husband, your confidante
Be my lady. Be my freak. Be my friend

ATOMS ABLAZE

Of cosmic romance scripted in papyrus scrolls
Gifted souls, two halves of an infinite whole
A love of profound reasons
Destined to imitate the phoenix
Like many lives before dictating this spiritual thesis
I adore all the more
You set me ablaze
A flaming passion melting my thermostat of resistance
Once listless now full of life
These eyes of mine are useless without you
My intellect futile without you
Your conversation is sustenance to my essence
Baby, I need you and love it
Ignoring me shoots pangs of terror throughout my body
Shockwaves crushing my bones leaving me flaccid and empty
Along an abandoned shore I reside
There's a flood behind my eyes
Building with each passing moment I'm unable to caress your face
Brush my fingertips lightly across your crow's feet
Like the strings of a harp
I need you and love it
Looking into space I wonder which star is ours
Disappointed by day baffled where the stars go
Similar to an optical illusion
Forever present beneath a transformation tantamount to suffocation
I'm being subjected
Escape with me into the distance the privacy of a fjord where your
mask is no more
Proving that the stars beneath never left only shadowed
By an instinctive defense mechanism
I overexert conveying there never being enough pay to encourage
falter of this heart
Nor my willingness to give minus rations
Inflamed surreal passion incomprehensible my lava is on the rise
From our essence sparks currents a breath to the campfire

Fragments of sapphire divine jewels of the cosmos
We're pieces of Mars, Venus, and all planets I suppose
Perhaps it's the pendulum of purity and pain
That penetrates your retina beckoning this risk taker yet subtly
heckling me when close
Baby, forgive me but I'm in it for the long haul
A glimpse behind the mask became my panacea
Dissolving the ache injected into my bones
If indeed I've succeeded at demolishing it into miniscule particles
Then who dares to reconstruct it
Precipitating fright within bringing a genuine smile to its end
Where the nostalgic begins

A GLASS OF AIR

The life of the romantic is never easy
To be such means that I will have to reveal parts of me
I've been concealing in safekeeping, for the risk exposure brings
For instance, she tells me that I'm too introverted and that I should be
more open
But when I explain I'm in love with her soul she immediately pushes
me away
Telling me that what I feel isn't real
That because with my situation comes a limited selection of women
That I'd basically fall for any woman thus am confused
I wonder if there could possibly be some truth to this
So I closely examine the validity of these emotions
I mean come on, who wants to dress fantasy in reality's attire, only
to be stripped naked by time (truth) finding one's self feeling like a
miserable fool
No, I refuse to wear the shoes of the bamboozled, rather treat fantasy
like underwear
Wearing the same pair for only a short while never a lifetime
Lest I remain silent allowing this divine opportunity to pass me by
It is necessary that I be assertive in alleviating my heart's wails
For two people from two different worlds to have so much in common
In addition to like aspirations, not to mention the chemistry of multiple
chemicals
How can we not consolidate in the furtherance of mankind?
Ostensibly, so much could be accomplished should we do so
There's no height we could not reach; no degree of happiness we
wouldn't know
Baby, I'm not concerned with those other guys or those other women;
all I desire is you
I've been crippled by fear of interpersonal relations for most of my life
Consequently, have experienced the likes of various women of
different ages
I'm ready for something adult
For the past few years I've had this picture of the ideal woman inside
my head

The trappings of the search trampled my heart
Just when I wanted to succumb along came you
The generation gap between us utterly insignificant
I commit wholeheartedly
Moreover the entire age thing is nothing more than a man-made
ideology
To which I do not abide

UN-FREEDOM OF SPEECH

I speak on ghetto life courts call it confession
Then sanction my crucifixion under broad discretion
Don't know me from Adam claim I'm viciously vested
The Lord expressly contradict 'em when he touch me with blessings
They plot our demise – oh you'd rather talk when I'm sober
Think I'm pretentious too suspicious of the snakes in these cobras?
Claim I'm mentally ill since I peg 'em as fascist
Who plot and scheme to keep us without financial status

FOR SPUR DOG

Today is glorious, so smile and smile big, as we don't get many days
such as this
Imitate the sun
Move in silence and remember the sun is on our side; it sees all yet
tells nothing
I can only aspire to be such – silent, efficient and forever in motion
I detect the same in you
Today is one of reflection and foresight; may it, too, prove memorable.
We are soldiers born of kindred hearts to survive in this cesspool
Where time's smiles go uncharted yet sought through abysmal pain
What you feel, I, too, endure.
So smirk with two middle fingers to the globe
For today belongs to you…happy birthday

TRUTH HAS MANY ENEMIES

My adolescence smothered by stress I kept pressing on
Learnt my lesson peasants wanna see us dead and gone
Struggling for years broken spirits in a poor existence
Rather perish than be in prison with male bitches
Try to lift people it's hard, genocide had me addicted
Could it be my forte to die in prison with lone rider's eyes on enemies?
Fight with strength of my forefathers
Brothers will continue to be converted to dead bodies
Until the day we sabotage Illuminati secret societies
This government try to twist us for sure they gonna get us
Because we breed outlandish wishes
It's time to heed as a people with open eyes
Visualize the hood without crack but decent jobs
Besides the fact our intellect topples jails
They fear the day we unite and rebel

MAN-HOLE

We quick to tell our spouses we love 'em
While our babies feel abandoned cause we fail to hug 'em
I can't say what it feels like to live lavish
Would love to say something to make you smile
But all my stories are tragic
My predecessors' successors left centuries of lessons
Don't know if I'll live past the pain yet so easy to promise aggression
Rather perish than proceed in a life of lies
What good are dominant genes when our destiny is an untimely demise
Courts claim me guilty ballistics failed to confirm
I flash a smile to my mother to appease her concern

HOPELESS

Got love for you Sista can't watch you fall to pieces
I know circumstances give all the reason
Behind on rent plus yo' baby is sick
Callin' on yo' mama for help knowin' she ain't got shit
You sent letters to prison – thanks for thinking of me
Said life would get better when it was too murky to see
You give me meaning; help put my life into focus
Seen a king in me when I was broken and hopeless
I try to reciprocate but you say my money illegal
Baby I've changed, aim to do right by people
I got your back when life sucks; slide a few grand beneath your pillow
While you cry on my shoulder
I make your enemies mine dreadful sight o' my pistol
You sigh I'm too much but give the word and I'm with you
They don't know the depths of our heart be forever uncanny
Endured blow after blow by the grace of God still standing

HINDSIGHT

Son, there's nothing bad about being angry
If used in the right way, anger could drive us to right wrongs and
correct injustices
Know that anger never changes, but we as people do have the capacity
To choose whether our individual anger will work for or against us
Think of the pilots on the stove. You turn a knob and fire appears, right?
Okay, now high or low it's still fire, right?
But son, your control of the knob controls the flames
Dry your eyes and control your knob, son

…AT BEST

Chest expanded, walking the yard with a mouthful of lies
Referring to guys as women, "she", "her", and blindly the mind is
conditioned
Prison garb worn in such a style that highlights one's stagnant position
Dismissing superstition so the cell has undergone transition
And is now called home and contentment
Opposed to hell and resentment – institutionalized henchmen
The mind-set is teeth-clenching
Refusing to fight that which doesn't bleed
So freedom is too distant to be seen
There will be no sowing of seeds, opposing the beast
Sadly, there will be no unity
The content of conversation goes unchanged "he said" "she said"
gossiping tongues untamed; itching to get to a different prison because
they serve hot dogs
A place where thousands of thriving minds are prostituted and
shackled
Institutionalized at best

SO I LIED

Here I am again
Compelled to place my fingers on these keys
Conducting the same process that drew me into you
And dispensed the keys to my foundation
Dumbfounded was I at the first words revealing your heart
But I could have made it through unscathed yes I could have
Had it not been for that last line
That haunting line
In one word she's poetry
To be thought of as such preceded by the honored designation
One of life's rarities
A moment such as I've never known
Reminiscent of a movie's montage scene
Scattered moments images dialogue interactions mocking smiles frowns
Culminating in the recollection of one intimate moment shared
I was paralyzed
All of these things running through my mind concurrently
Resulting in an explosion of emotion I had no choice but to deny
Deny deflect discourage discount demean deplore disapprove
Ignore it and it will go away they say
Hah
Not true say you your actions only intensified
More words thrust upon me and I am helplessly impaled
Your sword searing into me trapping me eternally
A man lost discovers destiny
It is I who is lost now
Lost inside the seductive depths of your mind
How can you be there inside me my every reflection my every
sensation?
Is it because you truly are in love with my soul as you so eloquently
convey
Mirror images from parallel worlds
Almost worse than realizing one is being manipulated as a game piece
Is realizing jarringly that there is no game being played
Or none as sinister as imagined anyway

Realizing that the surprise of discovery was mutual
Onward we plunge into the precarious mine field
Maneuvering carefully knowing any moment our merged world could
be razed
Making each moment more precious than the last
Parameters continually set and broken
Incapable of resisting the magnetic field corralling us
We risk
We surrender
We love

TRUST IS NOT A FOUR-LETTER WORD

Pain inflicted however unintentionally
Lays bare the inner child
Once thought healed and grown
But only lying dormant waiting for the trigger
That brings the quivering wailing entity forth
If I trust you with that intricate part of me
Don't make me regret my involuntary decision
Cherish me trust me nurture me heal me love me
Don't betray that reluctant trust I've placed in your heart
As you don't want me to betray yours
Understand I'm in as deeply as you are
Even if I'm doubly reluctant to display it
From hardened cast iron to soft malleable gold
So it is from crude strength to a yielding precious substance
Outwardly weaker but higher in value within
My strength is your strength
Your power is my power
Serendipitously drawn together from meandering paths
Together we are neither the pessimist's half-empty nor the optimist's
half-full
But filled beyond the capacity of our fused vessel

ON PERFECTION

Even the most perfect woman is imperfect
The most perfect relationship imperfect
If perfection can be captured then it must reside within imperfection!
So I guess that makes you perfectly imperfect
While effortlessly being imperfectly perfect
Meanwhile, within this unshakeable imperfection
My love for you, green eyes, is perfect

A SKY IN THE GROUND

Engaged in felonies for fear of being yellow
My criminal mind
Praised, rage with jealousy of Othello
Protecting it to the death forthwith my destruction
Brought solitary scars that became a group
About a countenance once handsome, perhaps not
My criminal mind
Inoculated apostasy for family
Sky is falling but I cannot look up
Instantly a thundercloud became me
Convincingly lonelier now pains me
I am the rock in rock bottom
The void of the abyss
The unsatisfying itch in rich
Still itchy palms write this
Clear skies are forecast
The storm passed
On to me there is no quick fix
But does ambition profess a criminal mind exists?
Even when I'm looking down I'm looking up

RUFF TUFF & DIRTY

A small child
I cruised with you
Public transit
Dilapidation
Graffiti
Addicts
A city…
Hopelessness showcased, roaches
Crawling in baby's crib
Your eyes bloodshot
Glazed by your favored drug
Dry snot blankets my top lip
Then a thumb licked
And my lip revealed
I cringe wiping at my nose
Turning my head away
Guess I'd rather be snotty
Than spit on
Rummaging through your purse
Stick of gum
Split it?
Sure
I'd sit beside you, wide-eyed
Swinging my legs, left shoe untied
Strings unraveled like lives on that bus
Hadn't understood the high
You escaped to
But sensed change in you I may have taken advantage
You *were* much nicer

EMERGING BLIND

Colonize states hungry for profit
Destroy life, regard for none
No 9 to 5 robbed banks, no problem
Done all on the low
Never advertise
Illegal adventures
Of one with illegitimate credentials
Monopolize street corners
Lives summarized under seventeen years
From street game to literati
Conspiracy to commit
To perusals of Illuminati
Once illuminated to return to darkness
Is to crack a blind eye
Who shall be blind with sight?!
It was the dark
Blinding my vision
Precipitating collisions
Ending in genocide
Beginning inside my mind
Remorse happened only at the slaying of my own
Still I haven't recovered
Smother emotion for others
In my pillow lies peculiar comfort
Barely can I lift my head for breath
Stench of my internal into external
Paralyzing…the mere transition!!!

POCKET LINT

All I ever wanted
Diametrically opposes all I've gotten
Who am I to ask why?
Instead of rolling with punches
I punch back
So rambunctious point they
Shy smile my reply
Hey, after all, life isn't fair they say
Precipitating or due to
Prejudice in man
I'm not sure
But am certain of a single thing
I am a winner
Even when treated like dirt
Leaves falling onto my chest
Birds mistaking me for the baňo
I am a winner
Hey forget you man!
Even my girl knows my worth
Worthy of her love
Directs me towards autonomy
If ever I fall weak
Though today things are bleak
I recall once winning a spelling bee
And hey, unlike me
Those kids were straight A students

WITHIN JUSTICE WE RISE

Our constitution
No more than an object in the rearview mirror
Much longer than today's credence
Yet minimized and trampled
An unyielding foundation
Sustaining centuries of pounding
Now malleable and meaningless
Beyond that elite few
No man is equal
Merely sub-human
With our conscience, compassion and such
Forbidden to marry whom we choose
Forced beneath laws of others' religion
Inner city populace subjected to unconstitutional positions
No one listens except to propaganda
Treacherous smoke screen of the wisest brains
Freedom existing merely ideally
And we're split from that
Liberation sought
Like those after our demise
Another word on inner cities
Particular profiling established
The established order's attempt at reconciling imbalance of races
Confined to races minus finish line
How then is a race held minus competitors?
Why do government agencies impose gang injunctions about ghettos?
Environment which its inhabitants cannot escape?
Forbidding American citizens to be caught in numbers beyond two
Jailing folks for spending time with family
Only to be taken into custody
Thrown inside cells filled with other assumed gang members
Obviously such injunction becomes moot once inside
But what does it all mean?
The stripping of human rights the lying to the masses
To what sort of justice are we confined?

What kind of government hovers over us?
Who's to say once a gang member always…
Who retains the right to continually punish those for decisions made at
twelve
When twenty-five and changed?
Somehow I manage to lift self above
Paradoxically within – justice

FIGURE 8

Mother yells
Calloused, I cringe not
Ignorance echoes throughout
Bounce about walls
Absorbed at my being
Pain into anger
Hurt begets antics immoral
The child, my sullen root
Picked apart and mishandled
Abused, forgotten
Dubbed rotten and confused
Older now, self is small
Chronologically mature, infantile still
Must sleep around
Around and round
Till self-loathing dissipates
Definitive moment
I'm said to have fathered a seed
Oh but fate is far too sinister
Far too perplexed to be so simple
Besides, I was much a jerk then
Hey lady, that's not my baby!
I could never father
See, my father, miscreant he
Miss-created my home
Deprived me of his touch
Then I my own
My resolve once wavered
As the world in flux
One thing done in accordance my micro-environment
The extension-depriving another seed with social encumbrance
Rifling his order at the outset
Stifling him
Sustaining a cycle

FIRST TIME RESPONSIBLE

- I feel guilt for having taken part in gang violence
- I feel guilt for taking my deceased cousin and uncle's existence for granted, and though I know that I love those dudes, I am not sure if I actually allowed myself to appreciate them while they were living even though we did spend time together.
- I feel guilt for spending more time with gang associates than with my own family.
- I feel guilt for not giving my younger siblings a chance to really get to know me, as I was basically raised in the system.
- I feel guilt for not taking full advantage of the opportunities I had to sit and really speak with my mother.
- I wish that I could go back and right so many of my wrongs because a lot of it wasn't done out of intentional ill will.
- I feel bad for not taking responsibility and having a blood test/ DNA test to find out if Tray is, indeed, my son; of this I feel the most guilt because I may have perpetuated the cycle that I am so bent on breaking.
- I feel guilt for selling crack to not only my people but people in general.
- I feel guilt being asleep on my feet for so damn long.
- I feel guilt for feeling sorry for myself and for doubting myself when I know that I am worthy.
- I feel guilt for procrastinating.
- I feel guilt for not being as explicit and open as I know I can be when conveying my thoughts, feelings, and ideals with the woman I love.
- I feel guilt for having shared that last part.
- I feel guilt for having subjected people to victimization.
- There come times when I'm alone and I think of some of what I've witnessed in the streets and begin to break down and cry, cursing myself, this life and wishing that things weren't the way they are. But my life is what it is and I know that the only way I can make things right is by changing

me then the conditions of my people. That's the only way I know how to make amends with my past; so yeah I feel guilty. Hell, I know I'm guilty of a lot of things, but what am I to do? I can't change the past, the things I've done and haven't done, I can't change that; so what am I to do?

EL GRITO DEL FLOR

Her cries floated to him on winter winds. From the warmth of the cabin he peered through the dewy window out into the dense forest, searching for a sign of her. And like always there she sat against the huge tree, which seemed to be consoling her. Though distance had a way of obscuring her face, he thought her beautiful. The way she sometimes danced beneath her favorite tree, to music only she could hear was alluring. Oftentimes he found himself gazing at her without courage to approach.

But today would be different, he told himself. He had been with many women in the past yet had not known love. A life of crime had that effect. But after years in prison, he'd shed the old and developed into a new person – searching for a new life; for that which makes the heart tingle. He fought and he fought to muster the nerve to tear himself away from his refuge and make her acquaintance. But seeing her weep was infuriating, and if that wasn't enough, nothing more than a silk nightgown protected her from leaking clouds. Something must be terribly wrong. Perhaps that was the impetus that sent him dashing out the front door, grabbing his heavy parka from the couch on the way; navigating the thicket with only one goal, one desire. He needed to make things right for her. If only he could destroy the source of her pain; if only to see her dance again, then everything would be fine. The rain had gotten heavier making it difficult for him to see. But never did he take his eyes from her. Less than twenty feet away his running became a brisk walk. His heart pounded against his chest the incessant beat of an ancient ritual. It was then the woman looked up and into the eyes of this stranger, who hadn't alarmed her in the least. And without a word he knelt, draping the jacket across her back and shoulders before helping her to her feet.

They stood there for a moment unsure of what to do next; he, shirtless, the rain glazing his chiseled torso like a hot pastry; while her wet body shivered against the wind's blows. Strands of lovely dark hair jealously clung to her face – and he understood. Just as he decided to speak, the heavens burst with deafening thunder. Seeing his lips mime his thoughts, she smiled. With an arm across her shoulders, they instinctively ran for his cabin, where she stood in front of the fireplace holding the jacket tightly around her like rainwater dripping from an exquisite sculpture; gliding down shapely legs. The rain, the fire combined was ethereal. He brought a blanket and a fresh pair of socks for her bare feet, then it was off to the kitchen where he retrieved the only bottle of wine purchased some six months back when he moved there, some chardonnay. After popping the cork, he poured two glasses. For the first time he noticed the way that the night gown accentuated her figure, the way that the water made it cling to her like a layer of skin. The sheer fabric was so revealing that he almost dropped the bottle and glasses. She pretended not to have noticed the way his eyes caressed her from head to toe and didn't quite understand how she could have such an effect on a man so handsome.

They sat on the soft, deep sea blue carpet, side by side, staring into the crackling flames. The woman with one of the small sofa pillows wrapped in her arms, the glass of chardonnay in her fingers, described the recent passing of her grandmother, the only family she'd ever known. He knew she needed an ear and thought it best to focus entirely on listening; only giving feedback when necessary. He wanted to convey his emotions, the way he often dreamt of her dancing in his arms, of loving her and only her, but thought it far too selfish. Neither had noticed the sun go down. Occasionally their eyes would lock; the chemistry as intense as electrical currents and flowed just as smooth. It was impossible for them not to feel it, this product of destiny; the workings of mythical goddesses. They sat and talked deep into the night. What he initially dismissed as a minor cough rapidly progressed into something much worse. Stoic, he dismissed it further. Their conversation evolved just as fast, with each sharing fantasies and their ideal mate. The woman knew that hers was sitting beside her. Unconsciously, she covered his hand with her own atop his knee. His eyes went from the fire to that in hers and scooted even closer, resting his head in her shoulder, thinking that her scent strongly resembled night-blossoming jasmine. Reluctantly, his eyelids fell with every cough. She sniveled. He died.

Through his stories and poetry Trayzon Akanaton seeks to inspire young people to choose a different path than the one which led to his incarceration.